shades of blue

First published 2020 by The Hedgehog Poetry Press

Published in the UK by
The Hedgehog Poetry Press
5, Coppack House
Churchill Avenue
Clevedon
BS21 6QW

www.hedgehogpress.co.uk

ISBN: 978-1-913499-24-2

A CIP Catalogue record for this book is available from the British Library.

shades of blue

Lucy Crispin

for Tony and Christine Crispin

contents

a libation for small things

These things have sorted themselves, somehow,
into the same place in my mind, a place
not so much lit, exactly, as not utterly black—
as when, in no matter how large a space,
a single candle alters the absoluteness of dark.

That lobelia lives there, self-sprung from last year's
window-box, pushing its white-hearted
sapphire-startling single bloom up
through the crack in the grey pavement
on the same street where a solemn child

stands steadily regarding me, staunch
in his Spiderman pyjamas, a local colossus,
red wellies planted, arms folded across
his chest. He is unencumbered by himself,
like the girl who skips from the shopping centre

on white-socked legs, out of the fluorescent blare
into a clear-falling, indigo April dusk,
her mother bustling but the little girl skipping
and singing out her greeting, *hello Mr Moon!*
And then there is the way the sun,

rolling down a winter sky of cautious blue,
suddenly backlights the moss which pads
the top stones of the lane wall, so that the slim
stalks which rise from the soft plump green
are red-gilded, alchemised by light;

or the way the blackbird is making a pulpit
out of the telegraph pole, threading all time
along his song and into this moment: now,
falling into forever; a beatitude of song.
And of course there is you, and the way,

as you sit cross-legged on the carpet, intent
on programming my new telly—the one I've
neither will nor patience to understand—the way
I see back through telescoped years to where
a small boy, ungrazed by time, is rapt in story.

And when delight or tenderness flower, thus,
in my throat, the tears are a libation for small things,
and how they reach us. Changing no worlds,
they change them entirely: a miscellany of handholds
—a way, in fact, to keep breathing.

January sends a short but important memo

We climb slowly along the winter valley's side,
cold enough to welcome the blood thud of walking,
warmed, too, by the rhythm of talk and no talking
which good friends have: communion-hunger satisfied,
the soul re-oriented, in centripetal
motion. We turn at the track's end by the old hall
to see a twin black sleekness of birds, distant-small:
two cormorants at the mere's edge, where skeletal
trees, coppiced into base-bunched clumps, are precisely
mirrored in the cloud-bright water. A bird leaves;
opened by the soft prow of its breast as it cleaves
the water; a single, perfect, widening vee
of wake. We pause, notice how the wall's moss glows
with the light it gathers; how deep the silent air goes.

the Bank Holiday Blues
to the tune of 'Onward Christian Soldiers'

It's the Spring Bank Holiday, folks are stepping out.
What if you are single? What's the day about?
Cars of laughing people speeding out of town:
sunny lives so wholesome you could gun the bastards down.
> *Oh! It's the Spring Bank Holiday,*
> *folks are stepping out.*
> *What if you are single?*
> *What's the day about?*

DIY's a no-no: Focus is too crammed.
Couples' home-improvements make your life seem bland.
Cursed unwonted sunshine tempts the lovers out
to the parks and cafes, where they put it all about.
> *Oh! It's the Spring Bank Holiday...*

Garden centres, stately homes, lakes and hills and fells
full of jolly people doing jolly well.
Bitterness invades your soul, misanthropic spite;
eat a tub of ice-cream, it will get you through the night.
> *Oh! It's the Spring Bank Holiday...*

TV's too depressing: you can always tell
only you are watching "specials" filmed in hell.
Music just reminds you of a better time
when you were not single and the holidays were fine.
> *Oh! It's the Spring Bank Holiday*
> *folks are stepping out.*
> *What if you are single?*
> *What's the day about?*

sea glass

'Due to weather conditions, the evening boat is cancelled.'
Under the risen wind, the waves' alternate push
and tug unfurls, rolls back, returns again,
while underfoot the shingle shifts and seethes,
a living ground which slides away from me
with a rasping rattle, like hard-won breath.

Graceless, I flail towards the frilled edge
where the foamed sea unrolls itself in greeting.
Sand swirls in the shallows, litter bobs,
and lank fingers of torn weed trail and clutch at me.
But beyond, the deeper reaches free me: I fall forward
into heaven-pale blue-green water which holds

and lifts me—where light is delighting in itself,
and the breeze-beaten surface is a shifting infinity
of tiny planes where sun is shattered into stars.
I blink brine-burned eyes and gasp, spitting salt;
a joy rises in me which joins now with far ago,
where a small child is tossed in sure square hands,

and squeals, and is caught again, and danger
is always safe. I laugh, and weep, and play
till I am spent. Leaving the water, I stoop to lift
a piece of sea-glass. Tumbled into opacity, it holds
the light. Carefully I fold my fingers over it,
its warm smoothness sweet against my salt-scoured skin.

four morning poems

the early birds

You're out early enough to take the folded daisies for stones
scattered through the grass;

they gleam dully under the nail-paring of moon
which rides down the morning sky.

Stealth blackbirds on steep ascents
whirr up from the track before your feet;

trees lift bare arms to the indigo glow
like celebrants, or infants waiting to be dressed.

Then to the east the sky is a lava lamp
where cloud blobs bob, grey on pink:

you notice how quickly light grows,
brings moment swift upon moment

and as the path becomes more definite—
further from the last dark, nearer to the next—

your step quickens. Birds *chuck-chuck*
in the emerging woods. All of you,

up early; catching the worms.

subject to gravity

Like a soft, high chord on a piano
or a *pianissimo* shimmer of strings

a white chiffon mist has been shaken out
across the valley and hangs there

oblivious to the coming hours
which are being forged

in the astonishing molten orange sky
behind the eastern hills. That held-breath

moment, the parabola's high point:
the unbearable beauty of beginnings

and your heart's prayer for exemption,
that you might stay and never drop

out of those incandescent crucible heavens
into the merely blue.

the unlikely faerie
or
on walking across the golf course before dawn, not keeping to the permitted footpaths

Soft droplets kissed my face and hair:
the dim and water filled the air
and made the world entire my place
though wide about me stretched green space;

and almost sure I was not seen
I cut a caper on the green.
In brief and silent revelry,
all trespass-sweet and just for me,

I leapt and whirled: my maypole was
the flag: I circled it because
I could, and antic pleasure found
thus secretly on velvet ground

in skipping on my booted feet;
and laughed an inward laugh full sweet
to know how Members soon would find
in dew the prints I left behind

but never know who thus with dance
besmirched the solemn turf. No chance
of retribution for the glee
I stole while darkness covered me.

But day is coming: through the gloom
familiar shapes begin to loom.
With private joy my eyes are lit
as homeward through the dawn I flit.

snow, three ways

(i)

A while till dawn. Breath plumes; your face,
slab frozen, and the ground ringing and glittering,
each grass-tongue frost-flicked, beautiful with cold.

Where the track skirts the copse you round the corner
to see white (cloud or snow?) piled against
the moon-washed indigo denim sky. Your heart
loosens, stirs at its moorings.

A few steps more and the hills reveal themselves,
pearl-pale not of this earth glimmer-earth,
their crescent line cupping the west and
(with the moon's gleam) saying, *will you?*

so that a gasp escapes you as your heart lifts free,
consigned to the world again—consenting, somehow,
without your consent.

(ii)

It seems so unstoppably confident
as it tumbles out of deepest navy
through the streetlight's nimbus—
flaring white, yellow, white again—
bringing stillness with it
(for we have not made it)
and time with it
(for we have not chosen it)
yet when it hits the pocked grey
patchwork of pavement
lapsing first into translucence
then slipping into nothingness
(we are bereft)
as though it had never been.

(iii)

Minutes from sun-up, and the air waits,
charged and tingling with snow-silence.

The bunch and flare of thistle heads,
the curve-cupped cones of teasel

and every spiral spike of hawthorn:
all are emphasised, outlined in this white

which crouches in wall crevices,
flings prodigal beauty over the slope of fell.

Now the sun rolls over the rim of the world
and newborn light warms the snow

with a glittering rapture of rose gold,
so that for this space between breaths

your heart's unquenchable thirst
is slaked after all, held in beauty

like the frozen drops which hang there
—look, just there—at every junction

of the ash tree; there, in her grace swoop,
dipping and bowing to the dazzling earth.

"well, everyone feels better when the sun shines, don't they?"

This isn't helpful, nor yet even true.
Some mornings when the curtain's rimmed with light
a dread arises in me at that bright
bold beckoning: the awful gape of blue
above, and how it hollows streets—how glass,
blank, parries sun, and air keeps everything
quite separate, and even birdsong sings
of gulf between what might be and what is.
And where I'd be instead is some high pass,
a stone-scrunch plod up through soft cloud; white, low,
gently populating the air with slow
shapes, hiding all but this near, russet grass,
this blue-green lichened rock: where peace renews
me and I need not bear the longer view.

it happens

Fallen for a charmer? Once in a while
you want to soak it up: the potent blue
eyes, the easy grace, that wonderful smile.

It's usually when life seems to pile
on the crap that, weakened, you crave things true
and simple: *please, just this once in a while*

let things be easy, let there be no guile
in the world, or calculation. So you
let yourself be charmed—blue eyes, gentle smile—

and then lose yourself in fantasy (hell,
it's better mapped than life), wildly dreaming you
can charm this charming prince but all the while

knowing, too, you should be running a mile
from such prodigal beauty. Join the queue
for the blue-eyed, charming, wonderful smile.

And so, tears before bedtime. Denial
of touch and love leaves scars that run right through.
You crave the wrong things and, once in while,
let blue eyes charm you from your wondering smile.

shades of blue

beach

Cloudy blue-green like sea glass
at the shingle beach
where men—serious, purposeful—
are buttressed by gear:
feet planted wide
astride the air,
they prime harpoons
and strap on bags for catch
before backing on flippered feet
into the water
like evolution in reverse

while, further out in the waves,
a middle-aged woman
is splashing a stiff-armed, awkward crawl,
throwing a stick every so often
then swimming to it,
as if she were her own dog;
and this puzzles me
until I see her emerge:
how she steps across the rocks and pebbles
sure-footed, leaning on the stick;
how when she has dried
the heavy breasts,
the beautiful, time-sagged flesh,
she dresses and, leaving the stick,
walks up the beach
towards whatever the day holds next.

high surf

Red flag whips
but the clear turquoise
wind-flexed
sea muscle
rolls, unfurls into foam:
water-lace laughing.
Come and play
it says,
shattering itself
over black rocks
into shards of light.

prayer on boarding the speedboat for an excursion

Oh Theia of the light blue view
I long for rapture into you:
might I arrive at yonder, I
would disappear where sea meets sky.

I beg, translate me into blue
as deep as distance, always new,
that I might rest—let time wheel by—
as unassailable as sky;

let ceaseless motion furlough grant
to this exhausted mind and heart
so that, as boat churns snow from sea,
I lapse into infinity.

On bended knees of thought I ask
relief from loving's endless task
and pray I might be lost in you,
sweet Theia of the light blue view.

noon

Like a cataracted eye
the sky is milky,
full of time.
It presses silence down
over the village.

Lapis paint blisters
on shutters battened
against the heat.

Under cars the midday dogs
are sleeping, flat
on their sides,
legs straight,
surrendered.
Not even a tail is twitching.

pool

Infinity pool, tiled in sky blue and cornflower,
wedged into the side of a hill
where olives writhe and the buzzard is quartering:
a box where light and water dance together.

I float at its lipless edge. Air stretches
from here clear to the far horizon
where the ombré sapphire sea lies down
beneath a wedgewood heaven.

Heat brands my limbs, claims me.
Water takes my weight: I drift, or am still.
Emptied of everything, I gaze
into the faultless forget-me-not sky, slung

between blue and blue,
vanished into the long space
between breaths, touched by grace,
opened.

Sunday

Sunday morning stillness. Only a few dogs bark.
A cock crowing, a distant call of sheep;
the belled goats' clanking on the scrubby slopes.
From behind the hill the sun strokes pink and lemon
across a baby-blue sky. A caravan
of puffy, pure-white cloud is lit from below,
as though annunciation is taking place
somewhere over there, just out of sight.

In the tiny burial ground marble tombs jostle,
white and streaky grey. Crosses on top,
and stone cabinets where lights flicker
in filigree holders. In one,
battered Nescafé tins flank a silver-framed photo:
a middle-aged man in a once-smart jacket,
smiling out of some distant day
at someone off-camera. An ordinary man,
smiling in the ordinary sunshine.

And now, on this ordinary morning,
that extraordinariness we call love
finds a woman tending this grave.
Matter-of-fact, she fills a pot with water,
brushes detritus from the marble surface,
places a coil of incense. It uncurls
its blue-grey smudge across the scent
of jasmine from a nearby garden,
while from the far side of the gorge floats
the sound of Mass, the priest's voice
climbing, leaning, climbing again—
drifting across the valley, down the years.

the poet reflects on a trip to Morrison's

For the poet, what behaviour is meet?
Through whirling doors she too must pass to do
the shopping, for even such as she must eat.

Selecting carrots, eschewing rare fruits sweet
she goes, wishing folk took sonnets in lieu
of gold; but such behaviour is not meet.

Her vehicle once fuelled, along the street
the poet passes halting 'midst the queue
of fretting trav'llers who, like her, must eat,

and reaches her home. On the mat to greet
her, foul documents writ in red. Oh, rue
the day! Rend them? Such behaviour's not meet,

for then come bailiffs' men on swiftest feet
to carry off those goods they think they're due,
ne'er dreaming that the poet, too, must eat.

The realm supports her not. Nor drink nor meat
is vouchsafed her. Her mood waxes more blue.
For the poet, what behaviour now is meet?
The garret looms. Oh, how is she to eat?

what the dogwalkers in the wood don't hear me thinking

Oh, all that wise stuff about letting go?
Say it to me in May, when daffs wizen
and blossoms brown underfoot, and risen
wind whips the infant softness from beech, so
sun no longer backlights the lifting leaves;
and in my head I run, scream, try to cram
my raging rictus mouth with wrens' song, ram
my ears with soft rain, garlic, bluebells, breathe
to lungs' limits wings' shutter-clatter, grasp
the brief hawthorn musk, shout as violets
furl tired petals, rend heart with regrets
for what I haven't loved enough, can't clasp
or keep. Say all that wise stuff. I know it is so.
But I stand in this world, and I howl, and I say: no.

wormholes and paradox

"The Archaeological Museum of Chania welcomes the Gods of Aptera"
—museum poster, summer 2019

These stick figures, metal dulled brown,
are caught in clumsy beautiful *port de bras*,
left arms hooped out at chest height,
right hands lifted to the forehead: venerating.
Simplicity transfigured by honesty
they ask, out across four thousand years,
the usual questions: how should we live?
what matters? is there any help out there?

In another case, Roman mourners sit in stone,
old women spread with age, sheathed in scarves,
toes peeping out from beneath their skirts.
Their eyes are cast down, faces serious,
not sad; they are simply looking at the facts.
You can see that their hands clutch closed
their shawls from the inside; that they have sat
patiently, and long. Displayed nearby,
three flattened ovals of wire, thick with verdigris
and time—one end sharpened, the other
folded back on itself to receive the point—
are instantly recognisable: nappy pins.
Connection bolts, earths at my heart.

I sit at the museum's door, looking out
over the bleaching, sun-shocked garden.
Beyond it, the noon hour café hum, the roar
and jostle of the street; within, broken-off columns
stand in grass; a stone fragment of lion;
a mantle; our lunchbox, sitting on a Roman plinth.
Behind, a step away in the dim cool quiet,
this assemblage of wormholes and paradox:
how tiny we are, and how large;
how our lives mean everything and nothing at all;
how these things have always been true.

Gleaming in the gloom, Apollo and Artemis
are marble sleek, aloof and beautiful.
In a chair at their feet a teenager sits silent,
absorbed in her phone; not yet on the lookout
for gods to welcome. I reach for a sandwich
and notice the still-bright browns of a young sparrow
lying fallen in the dusty grass at my feet.

waiting to go back to the specialist

I'm enrolled at the School of Uncertainty,
rising promptly for lessons which today
take place here on the fell, out in the beautiful early.
Our topic this term is "Where We Live";
which is now;

accordingly, I heed how the ash shoots
spring gleefully from those late black buds,
loft leaves on limbs lifted in the shapes
of exultation, like charismatic preachers
giving glory.

I study the hawthorn, as bright and fragrant
as laundry, with its pink-tipped constellations
of stamens held in the smooth cups of white,
and observe, in its wind-shaped shade,
a hare, crouching,

the definition of attention as he checks the air
for news. I listen as the curlew's song
pours cool sweet water, a response to questions
about thirst, and grace; I note the small unfussy
brownness of lark

disappearing into the high all-holding blue
until only the strobe of sound remains.
Cowslip tannoys blare yellow into morning,
dandelion ghost globes offer silence
and I get it,

suddenly: how now will only ever have itself
to show me—is neither pacifier nor panacea;
does not solve a mystery but instead
invites us into it. I see how this must
be learned by heart,

and pause to log it, here in the building heat
where lambs and panting ewes have tucked themselves
into shade. The rumble of lorries rises
from the road below but has as yet, for them,
no particular meaning.

sea stones

They are never so beautiful as now:
lustrous with light and water,
a succession of small startles
shining in the dun matt sand.
Blown bubbles wander up
from the waveline, skate on waterfilm
which holds the piebald sky,
the adolescent April sun.
I walk on blue-white heavens.

I bend to prise up a pebble,
wipe wet sand from its underside.
This is my stone: a faded brown
with a perfect circle of grey
at one end, it's rough-smooth
like an egg, a perfect palm fit—
cool and comforting and sure.
Into my sagging pocket it goes.

At home, it will sit with others
in the bowl on the windowsill:
dry dull, sometimes dusted,
no longer recalling me to where I was,
or when, but only a reminder
that I have inhabited my days; and that
nothing is ever so beautiful as now.

acknowledgements

Some of the poems in this collection first appeared in *The Salopeot, Eildon Tree, Iceberg Tales, The Blue Nib, Channel* and *Poetry Birmingham.*

Like thoughts, thanks often lie too deep for tears... to the following people, named simply in alphabetical order, I offer my great gratitude:

Susan Allen, Rosie Bailey, Richard Barnes, Ken Blackie, Hazel Clarke, Jeff Cowton, Simon Davies, Mark Davidson, Celia Forsyth, Susie Gibson-Ross, Jenny Glover, Helen Grant, Meg Hill, Richard McHale, Suan Marston, Jane Maycock, Desmond Reaney, Edmund Stenson and David Thomas.

And all the members of *the 42 group* and the Kendal *What are Words Worth?* community.